Jeni Wood.
30 : VIII : 57 :

THIS BLIND ROSE

HUMBERT WOLFE

THIS BLIND ROSE

————————————

Humbert Wolfe

March 19/38

LONDON
VICTOR GOLLANCZ LTD
14 Henrietta Street, Covent Garden
1928

Printed in Great Britain by
The Camelot Press Ltd., London and Southampton

NOTE

The poems in this volume have been written in the last five or six years, but no attempt has been made to arrange them chronologically. A few of them are reprinted with permission from the *Atlantic Monthly*, the *New Statesman*, the *Irish Statesman*, the *Queen*, *Country Life*, the *Spectator*, the *Saturday Review*, and the *Nation*. Others which have previously been published have been so altered in re-writing that acknowledgment would be merely misleading.

H. W.

CONTENTS

7

CONTENTS

8

CONTENTS

CONTENTS

INVOCATION

INVOCATION

TAKE these, as you have taken,
   all my verse,
Muse, as a petal shaken,
   when your foot stirs
blooms Time has stolen
   in his long feud
with your unfallen
   white multitude.

HEADPIECE

Rose, be a parable, when love's afraid,
of how things fadeless, when they seem to fade,
concede to death, the Cæsar, being his,
only their temporal errors, as hostages.

Tell him your beauty, before Eve's heart was wrung
with the sly apple, was as old—and young ;
tell him in Troy, tell him in Lyonesse,
it could have been no more, it was no less.

Tell him your shape, some god made in the image
of the song the Sirens sang, suffers not damage,
since Time to that divine conjecture must
remould, each spring, the instrumental dust.

Tell him, while winter with the thorn may gloze
each year the gospel of the risen rose,
a thousand Junes with all their buds present
to love your apostolic testament.

SERENADE

WHAT shall I say when I am old
   and the young men reading me
find in you only the crystal-cold
   graces of poetry ?

What shall I do when your beauty, for these,
   is legendary as hers
who was the womanhood of Greece
   made manifest in verse ?

What shall I do, how shall I prove
   against prevailing time
that rhyme endures because of love,
   not love because of rhyme ?

How shall I make them understand
   that all I do in this
is but to set against your hand
   a last unfleeting kiss ;

and not with words, but like a hare
   that crouches in her form,
my lips, for ever moulded there,
   will tremble and be warm ?

ARE YOU AFRAID?

ARE you afraid, now that the white moon blabs
  of her Endymion, and does not care,
though midnight with his sable dagger stabs
  the heart her love lays bare ?

Are you afraid, now that the quiet trees
  whisper behind their leafy lattice bars,
and throw them open on the first small breeze
  to entertain the stars ?

Are you afraid, when night is leaning over
  the dim Arabian earth, whose heart is laid
beating against the darkness of her lover ?
  Listen ! Are you afraid ?

SUBSTANCE

If flesh could lay aside her tricks
of substance, and we two could mix
without the body's intervening,
would love confirm or lose his meaning?

If thoughts divided, that surprise
the dawn which rose in other eyes,
discard at last the golden guess,
would that be love or loneliness?

If your rose-petalled difference
trembled no longer on my sense,
and separate beauty lost her touch,
had love won all, or won too much?

Too much, for how should lovers spell
in one decisive syllable
the myriad phrases of the grammar,
that even poets can but stammer—

stammer, and, when their lives are spent
in vain in that experiment,
are satisfied if they can prove
that poetry has learned from love

time in division, and the dark
enchantments of the broken arc.
Too much, since love, like music, is
a sound between two silences.

RETURN

I HAVE come back not as a lover requited,
  nor making any claim, unless you deem it
a claim to walk with your reflection lighted,
  and share your dream of beauty as you dream it.

I am content to stand without the portal,
  seeing in the cool, pale meads of Avalon
my lover look back once from peace immortal,
  gravely, to where I wait, and so pass on.

For to have loved you is an action moulding
  all that I am, and setting me apart,
as though you were the spring, and I unfolding
  in silence like a flower in your heart.

And thus I am a part of you for ever,
  as Syrinx, though she fled from Pan, became
a reed that all day long beside her river
  murmured, and was the echo of, his name.

JUNE UNJUNED

LET what was said be all unsaid,
the prayer unprayed, unkist the kiss,
and June unjuned forswear the red
rose for the yellow primroses.

Before the earliest poppy is born,
let Time be green among the corn,
and let us tug him by the hand,
as once, and make him understand

that he is playing in a game
where each must guess the other's name,
and while we two are anything
we like, his name is always spring.

And then we'll sprawl, with hearts unwrung,
upon the grass, and hear how joy
died with love's pain, and think it sung
about some other girl and boy.

ROMANCE

Though it were long since,
    though it were past over,
it was romance,
    and deathless, my lover—

Fairy-horn that sounds,
    in no time and no land,
the immortal wounds
    of the Childe Roland,

Homer of Achilles,
    healing the light foot
with the long lilies
    of his flute,

and spring that was green once,
    letting her light fall
on love, that has been once,
    returning at nightfall.

LOVE

I WILL tell you what love is : Love is the broken
sound in the night of feet that pass. Unwoken,
the lover stirs in his sleep, and, while he stirs,
a foot has gone past in the night as light as hers.

I will tell you what love is : Love is the proud
mouth that was shut in marble, and the loud
songs of the world are sung on lips all warm,
but these cold lips sing not, and have worked such
    harm.

I will tell you what love does : Man builds a greater
city than Babylon with gardens, and love, turned
    traitor,
sells the high town to the dream's eternal foeman,
that comes with the false sweet key, by night, of a
    woman.

I will tell you how love ends : Without a sound
love stabs in the dark of the heart, and leaves no
    wound.
And what was a man goes slowly, listening
for a tune played on a harp, but it has no string.

I will tell you all these things, and when they are told,
I shall remember the austere head of gold,
his slender motionless grace, and how he stands
looking with happy wonder at the cowslips in his hands.

27

LET us be sure of this—
there's more in love than the kiss ;
there's more in love than taking
hands in the dark, and waking
quietly, to whisper over
love, and the name of the lover.

Let us be sure no less
that there's a last caress,
having a graver fashion
than the wild graces of passion—
that is neither given nor taken,
but waits for a god to waken.

Let us be very sure
that passion doth not endure ;
but love who, when he dies
must needs lose Paradise,
ends in a music spilt on
not even the lips of Milton.

HEINE

I THOUGHT of Heine, and of your sea-thrilled hair,
and of that least small movement of your mouth,
when the Northern words you speak home through the
    air,
steadily beating to the heart's dim South ;

and how he cried that the belovèd was too fair,
too lily-cold for love, too white to guess it,
and how he would have laid his hands on her hair
gently, as I do now on your hair, to bless it.

I LAY these lilies,
   goddess, this sheaf,
as once in happiness,
   now in grief.

If they are trembling,
   they trembled no less
with the burden
   of happiness.

Those were a coronal,
   these are a wreath,
but the buds are as stainless,
   as verdant the sheath.

For spring, like the Chinese
   sculptor's art,
has all of beauty
   save the heart.

Immortal lady,
   a mortal brings
these brief, but final,
   offerings.

GHOSTS

LOVE's a ghost, and no one knows
whence he comes and where he goes ;
for the hearts that he has haunted
could not tell us if they wanted.
Love's a ghost, and though he come
singing from Paradise, he's dumb ;
for all hearts when they beat near him
cannot, will not, dare not hear him.
Love's a ghost, and who can taste
lips through which the dawn has raced ?
Who can touch them, who dare part
lips, though closed, that draw the heart ?

And, since ghosts, belovèd, spill
with the dawn's first daffodil,
in the night, ere love be lost,
sweet, come out and find your ghost.

TWO GHOSTS

If I'm a ghost, and you're a ghost, and both of us are
    nothing else
than shadows, a moment lit and then all grey,
bells ringing to one another, and then hushed bells,
shall we be divided, shall we turn away?

Shall we be afraid, ghost, of our ghostliness?
But all love is a proud walker in a dream,
and all kiss shadows, shadows themselves, and press
to seeming hearts, hearts that as faintly seem.

We have met in a mist, and in a driving mist
have been together, and though in the mist we are lost,
at least we have touched a second, at least we have
    kissed.
What more had any lovers—ever—ghost?

THE HOUSE OF GHOSTS

First to describe the house. Who has not seen it
  once at the end of an evening's walk—the leaves
that suddenly open, and as sudden screen it
  with the first flickering hint of shadowy eaves?

Was there a light in the high window? Or
  only the moon's cool candle palely lit?
Was there a pathway leading to the door?
  Or only grass and none to walk on it?

And surely someone cried, " Who goes there—who? "
  And ere the lips could shape the whispered " I,"
the same voice rose, and chuckled " You, 'tis you ! "
  A voice, or the furred night-owl's human cry?

Who has not seen the house? Who has not started
  towards the gate half-seen, and paused, half-fearing,
and half beyond all fear—and the leaves parted
  again, and there was nothing in the clearing?

SILENCE

LET us be still. There is nothing that we can do
    as excellent as silence. All the night
you did not answer, when I cried to you
    for impossible consolations. You were right.

Like soft black snow, the darkness through the air
    fell in long flakes, that, heaping in the past,
hushed all the voices that had echoed there,
    and even your voice was quiet at the last.

I was afraid lest, sinking in the snow,
    a final peace might seal my tired eyes,
and I should dream that I was loved, and so
    awake in hell, to find the dream was lies.

Fool ! for who knows if, feeling like the spring
    back into winter, silence may not stir
the broken husks of love, that blossoming
    are in their resurrection lovelier ?

Who knows if silence may not be the line
    in which our patterns their intent renew,
and, with the imperfect music that is mine,
    restores the perfect cadence that is you ?

Who knows what silence is, who knows if we,
    that out of tumult into silence move,
may not be passing unbelievably
    out of love's earthbound shadow into love ?

FLOWERS, BIRDS, TREES, STARS,
AND THE MOON

THIS BLIND ROSE

As this blind rose, no more than a whim of the dust,
    achieved her excellence without intent,
so man, the casual sport of time and lust,
    plans wealth and war, and loves by accident.

OLEANDERS

WILL you remember only the oleanders
(Rose-bay, rose-bay, where are your roses now?),
and the still palm, and all spring's green pretenders
that claimed their kingdoms, when love breathed his
     vow?

Will you remember only the moon, deceiving
the trees with her cold dawn, some lucid eve—
will you on these alone be still believing
when there is nothing else you can believe?

Or, afterwards, when you look back on love,
will you remember how, by some tall hill,
he poised with wings that only seemed to move
because life lay unutterably still?

Will you remember only the upward flight—
the lasting stroke of beauty at a star,
when the whole world plunged downward into night,
but only plunged because love rose so far?

Will it be love between the flowers and the trees,
or love between the moon and mountains fair,
or will you think, instead of all of these,
on some small thing we never guessed was there?

40

Some daily happiness, some trifling anguish,
some usual gesture, stored within the heart,
that might assume, when life's great moments languish,
gravely the cool authority of art ?

Will you remember this or the oleander,
or will the years, when mine is still, endow
some stranger voice, that will not even wonder,
" Rose-bay, rose-bay, where are your roses now ? "

If God had given man the power
to warn the blade, and warn the flower,
" Death is the guerdon of all that live ! "
and they refrained—would they forgive ?

Would daffodil the spring desert
because her golden ballet-skirt,
poised on a slim green-stockinged toe,
with the first pirouette, must go ?

Would primrose lay aside her yellow
competition with her fellow ?
Would violet refuse to be
blue in spring's lapis lazuli ?

Would crocus timidly disclaim
her silver heart of candle flame ?
Would ragged-robin fail to make
her universal red mistake ?

And if the smallest flower or weed
demands her bright specific need,
and tosses death behind her stem,
are we too proud to learn from them ?

Are we afraid to tell the sage
(who warns us) that the heritage
of certain death, which does not fret
the uncourageous violet,

we shall accept, and, being heirs
to his disorderly affairs,
will teach him that a gentleman
will spend his credit while he can.

SINCE it is evening,
  let us invent
love's undiscovered
  continent.

What shall we steer by,
  having no chart
but the deliberate
  fraud of the heart?

How shall we find it?
  Beyond what keys
of boyhood's Spanish
  piracies,

false Eldorados
  dim with the tears
of beauty, the last
  of the buccaneers?

Since it is evening,
  let us design
what shall be utterly
  yours and mine.

There will be nothing
  that ever before
beckoned the sailor
  from any shore.

Trees shall be greener
    by mountains more pale,
thrushes outsinging
    the nightingale,

flowers now butterflies,
    now in the grass,
suddenly quiet
    as painted glass,

and fishes of emerald
    dive for the moon,
whose silver is stained by
    the peacock lagoon.

Since it is evening,
    and sailing weather,
let us set out for
    the dream together.

set for the landfall,
    where love and verse
enfranchise for ever
    the travellers.

CYCLAMEN

SHE rests. O do not bring again
           white cyclamen,
the flower like two butterflies
with wings across each other's eyes.
Drop rather by that quiet cell
snowdrop or daffodil,
lest the remembered fragrance stir
           the heart with her.

SPRING

THE sun-gold seas bank up, and spill
in leagues of ruffled daffodil,
nor brine, it seems, but woodland scent
aneles a lazy continent.

The sea-gull scrawls across the sky
the vivid patterns of her cry,
and, dipping swiftly, almost weaves
an azure tracery of leaves.

But, matching ocean's floral guess
at the earth's stable loveliness,
spring sweeps the wood's cathedral nave
with the green fury of a wave,

till oak and elm and beech and ash
in one viridian comber crash,
while at their feet red vetches shine,
sharp, and cold, and coralline.

And thrushes in the forest rides
flute echoes of the haunted tides,
where mermaid-birches, palely fair,
comb the sea-silver of their hair.

For thus each spring a god creates
the ancient world anew, and waits
each spring in vain for men to know,
if they would dare to dream it so,

all things may change and shift and melt
into the beauties they have felt,
and keep the shapes the dream has lent
by some immortal increment.

MOUNTAIN-FLOWERS

CLIMB by the path, and you'll find mountain-mallow,
  narcissus, restless in the wind, as though
she heard a voice beseech her bloom to follow,
  and softly drown in the reflective snow.

Or higher still, like little red macaws,
  in green sequestered cages, brooding, see !
the Alpine rose, obedient to the laws
  which rule that vertical mute aviary.

Then, last of all, only the edelweiss,
  not soft like any other flower else,
but a small cuttle-fish against the ice,
  clutching the rock with pale grey tentacles.

These and a thousand others, how small, how brittle,
  how easily pulled, how folded in the hand,
and how long afterwards a single petal
  is all we keep of vision's Oberland.

DR

THEY have said all things of you, nightingale,
   save this—that you, like all the rest
who sing through the passionate midnight, fail
      when song is loveliest,

when, like a juggler tossing at the sun
   a hundred torches, from your torchlit throat
you toss the coloured shadows of the one
      uncapturable note.

But, when you are suddenly silent, I hear that note,
   the same, I think, that Robert Browning heard,
when hands were laid over his eyes, and he wrote :
      " Angel ! " but wondered, " bird ? "

THE EASTERN BIRDS

THEY will cease crying presently—
those two gold-tufted Eastern birds,
released among the lilacs,
the moon-cold flame of the lilacs,
in spring, in a green garden.

They will cease crying presently,
when they are afraid no longer
of ghosts in the shape of flowers,
of scented ghosts like flowers,
that haunt in a tranquil sunlight.

They will cease crying presently
of that beauty under water
of the slowly-swinging lilacs,
through whose sea-blossom quietly
glide, as on wings, the grey bird-fishes.

They will cease crying presently—
as the Eastern birds of my love,
released among your lilacs,
your pale, dew-throated lilacs,
cease crying, and fold their painted vans.

HAREBELL

Lie easy, harebell ! Do not wither
quickly, as blooms that light hands gather.
But burn your little lamp of blue
steadily, all night through,
marking the small grave
where the joy that we did not have,
and the poem I might have made,
                are laid.

WADHAM GARDENS

SLIDES the dead
cedar-tree (almost
as under wave
a deep sea-ghost)
in the star-trembling
air of June.
Through the long
breakers of the moon,
as once they strode, now
swim to her
two owls, than fishes
quieter.

THE OLIVE TREES

GREEN sheep—the olive-trees—
climb patiently to the walls of the hill-town,
and higher still a line of cypresses,
with folded arms—dark-leafèd mutes—look down.

Someone has passed this way,
riding, as on that mule the peasant rides,
for the neat hoofs from the track never stray,
finding, no doubt, old prints, that daylight hides.

What cavaliers, how mounted, with cascade
of what clear bells, cooling the air, climbed slowly,
long since, in what forgotten dawn, and made,
merely by climbing, all the hillside holy?

Someone has passed this way, we guess,
since, climbing by their path, that wholesome mule,
that peasant going on his business,
flash immemorially beautiful.

VENUS

AND love will come when life has said, " It's late :
  he'll not be here to-night." And she will bar
the door, and rake the ashes in the grate.
  But the dark room will glimmer with a star

invisible by lamplight—Betelgeuse,
  or that Arabian lantern, whose tall name
bends with the light, as the twig the Chinese use—
  or let it be the star, whose smaller flame

bows not to those great torches, but, when no man
  remembers her, suddenly slips between us
and the silence in our heart—the splendid Roman
  lady they worshipped in the name of Venus.

Then, as when naphtha splashes at a fair
  its brilliant rust on the dark revellers,
so memorably bright on some girl's hair
  you'd say that it was Rembrandt's, and not hers,

this elfin beam, threading the daily thicket
  of sofa, chair, and table in flame, would wind,
distant and small and sweet, Childe Rolande's tucket
  from love's lost Roncesvalles, and stab the mind,

so that life, listening with a little crookèd
  smile to her heart, thus dabbled with the stars,
would yield to love on a sob, as Venus, naked
  in the unclouded deep of heaven, to Mars.

I STRETCHED out my hands to the birds on the wing.
   Easily they fled crying into the West.
But when there was quiet I heard them sing
   in my heart of the night that is best,

of how the stars are hidden by a cloud,
   of how the pale and pilgrim moon doth keep
so frail a candle in heaven, because she vowed,
   but could not wait, to hear Endymion weep,

of how she drifted down to her lover, pale
   snow, making immortal what its beauty blanches,
still as the snow in the voice of the nightingale,
   falling on the heart as the snow bends the branches.

VERSE AND MUSIC

A BAY-LEAF

I GIVE you back the bay-leaf, Shelley's leaf,
    that is not mine to wear, but yours, who found it.
For, though I stole your beauty, let a thief
    confess 'twas you, and not his song, that crowned it.

Let me return the bay, as, if I could,
    I would return all else—the days I stole,
and the moon's intercepted maidenhood,
    as silver and as silent as your soul.

Let me return the bay—not as a token
    that song has left me, but as knowing that
no verse of mine, but words you have not spoken,
    alone can decorate love's laureate.

Take the bay back. I will reclaim it when
    life sets your music to my minor key,
so that we hear, when it is played again,
    the undertones of immortality.

I will not wear the bays for less, nor you
    for less than this would have them on my brow.
But I will wear them, when that tune breaks through.
    Take back the bays—I will not wear them now.

WORDS

Now that I have nothing left
   but a word and another,
I shall take them in my hands
   and beat them together,
till they are words no longer,
   and even then
their perilous ghosts will
   rise again
out of the grave softly,
   to taunt me,
and with unbearable love-
   liness haunt me.

O beautiful words,
   how have I sinned,
that I have an ache for you
   nothing can mend,
that you shame my passion,
   and mock no less
sorrow, and quiet
   happiness
with the wonder, and
   little cry
of your eternal
   alibi ?

SONG

AND then there's song—that lane along the air
that lets a bird through to the heart—as though
there were a god's wings hidden in your hair,
and your lover saw them, and you did not know.

O silence ! you slow ghost, let your hands threaten
other men's dreams ; they shall not wicker in mine.
But word shall call to tilted word, and straighten,
as when two spans of a bridge clap, into a line.

Aye ! that is song—to beat the lark on the wing,
and to be first in heaven, to tumble faster
down the lost dreams than a stone, and yet to sing,
till love and dreams and death salute their master.

I HAVE loved violins, and I have thought as I heard
  them
  that they were birds, crying at the other side of the
  wood,
birds in the light beyond the dark wood, and none has
  snared them.
  I thought that they were birds crying, but I had not
  understood.

They were a shadow, but not of song beyond the world ;
  they were an echo, but not of invisible light.
They were love's first banners, tremblingly unfurled
  by standard-bearers, marching alone in the night.

They were the avant-posts, lifting their gold-pennoned
  lances ;
  they were the harness ringing of beauty's vedettes,
and they reined their horses at the dawn where romance
  is,
  where the heart remembers, but the fiddle forgets.

For the fiddle soars up, and is lost in its own
  silver cascade, that tumbles in rain,
out of the glory that it could not have known,
  back to the dark earth that it spurned in vain.

Violin, viola, viol d'amore,
  sing and are silent, but I, who guessed them
to be birds crying in some star-haunted story
  of magic beyond the world, yet I have blessed them.

For they have become the voice of my own heart,
    speaking,
  they have become that voice, and one voice dearer.
And they do not fall back to the earth, and there is no
    waking,
  but they shine and rise like a star, and the star draws
    nearer.

THERE have been greater poems
    than these are,
songs as imperious
    as gold Cæsar.

There have been other lovers,
    whose passion
swung into radiance beyond
    division.

Such poems, such lovers,
    I have read of.
But these poems, this love, are what
    the heart is made of.

THE SNOW AND THE CANDLE

As in the light of candles the fiddle renounces
    death and the dark for dancers, and conjures mad
      heartsease,
so, when the moon smokes upward, with rustling
    flounces
    the snow to some starry rebeck swan-glidingly
      curtsies.

Whisper the satins of the dark Genoese ;
    soft sigh on the air pale laces from France,
swayingly deep, till the wind shatters peace
    with adventure's beautiful violence.

His are shrill trumpets, deep drummers, beating :
    " Farewell to the dance ! Farewell ! O bright
      dancers ! "
and the hoofs of the horse, the heart repeating,
    when it knocks in the night, and no heart answers.

They danced under candles, they rode out, and were
      not,
    the loved and the lovers in all those eves,
and now the snow stirs for those who stir not,
    for those who grieve not, the high wind grieves.

They do not dance now, but the snow dances.
    They are only heard in the wind's tall scandals—
a sob in the snow, the wind's wild fancies—
    and the moon in heaven is the last of their candles.

LAST night flutes were playing,
but at the end I said :
" You are only the ghosts of music
exquisitely dead.
You have returned, you are haunting,
how palely, how thin—
memory, memory
that wanders in
out of the night into the heart.
It is easy," I was crying,
" for you to tremble, for you to enthral me,
as the dead draw the dying."

As always when he has finished writing,
he who takes the pencil out of my hand
looks at me with bright, half-wondering malice,
and says, " Another poem by Humbert Wolfe.
Well, take your poem, and make the most of it ! "
And at first, as I read the poem,
it is not my poem at all.
If it is a poem of mountains, it is as tall
and lovely as the mountains themselves.
There will be flowers (O gentians ! O gentians !
I saw you in sheets of blue, and I did not know your
    name,
but I said to myself, as a man says
when he sees the face of the chosen woman,
" This is for me and I for this,"
O gentians !)
Or, if it is a poem of life, then like a meadow,
under trees in moonlight, life lies, all dreaming
and still, save for the little moving shadow
of wings between the meadow and the moon.
But presently, as I read,
the words lose their dew, the green
and fragrant thoughts are gradually cloaked
with the dust of the common road
that all feet tread.
And the poem is just a poem like any other
that I have written.
And I give it a name, and sign it, reluctantly,
Humbert Wolfe.
But the true poem—the one that I have not written,
of which mine is the discarded husk,
is safe with him who wrote it,

and with the poets who, when this stranger smiled,
caught him by the wing, and, though they could not
    hold him,
found in their star-stained hands one golden feather,
which touched their page.

PLACES

GIRL, there were girls like you in Ilion,
   who, watching Helen, whispered, " A veil draws over
her beauty, that might have put the morning on
   like a tunic, and lo ! she spends it for a lover."

And in all the luminous cities after Troy,
   in the drugging arms of Time that deeply swoon,
these girls rejected, like the Grecian boy,
   love, and the pale addresses of the moon.

They hoarded their loveliness, while Helen spent it.
   They were young as the first crisp lily is young,
straight as the corn before the wind has bent it.
   But when are they named now, and where are they
      sung ?

They were enough to themselves, and denied
   the action of life. They lived, and are gone.
But Helen is for ever fair, and a bride.
   Girl, there were girls like you in Ilion !

I THOUGHT of a hill-road by Zweilutschinen or
    Chamonix.
  I thought of the pines that are as old as the snows,
and I thought of all time past, that I could not see,
    of the seed of the pine, and of the mountain that no
    man knows.

I was hurt in my heart, because it was mutable,
    and all these things, changing, change not at all ;
and the silence, when there is no wind in the mountains,
    fell
    as it has always fallen, as it will always fall.

There was not even the feather of a falling cascade
    to mitigate the quiet of the pines and of the hill.
I was alone with the hush, and I was afraid,
    because thus in the end, at the centre, all things are
    still.

There is no movement. Between nightfall and day-
    spring,
    action immobilised, like a sleeping rose,
swoons, and, since no man has passed that way, spring
    has no meaning, and the meaningless summer goes.

The flower is not a flower for men any longer.
    It has become its own thing, as action is its own,
when there is an end of thirst and of hunger,
    when the heart has surpassed itself, and is alone.

The heart has known love's value, and the power,
  and now love and pain are names it no longer knows.
There is something greater or less. Like a sleeping flower,
  life folds on itself and forgets, like a sleeping rose.

HERE, where all question ends,
    the unembarrassed height
indifferently spends
    youth and delight,

hope after fever laid
    at rest in spacious peace,
love, a bright renegade
    to loneliness,

and life, as frail as fickle,
    as little as the dark
person—the small brown freckle
    in heaven—of the lark.

Here there is naught as true
    in all the spirit of man
as, at his feet, the blue
    of gentian.

Here all he has of false
    is melted in the snow
of the cool-throated bells
    they swing at Caux.

Here triumph, here despair,
    each claiming the heart for hers,
die on the perfumed air
    between the firs.

Here, where all question ends,
    and heat is done, and strife,
night, her dark sister, bends,
    enfolding life.

WHERE are the leaves (he sang) of those dark trees
that did not shake in any wind man knows ?
Where do they lie, by what glass-tranquil seas,
or soft beneath what everlasting snows ?

They must have fallen when the last troubadour
drew in the night, under the milk of the moon,
into the hidden chaces, where naught was sure
save darkness, and the ending of the tune.

They must have fallen when the last dark Queen
of Tourney saw the last and youngest son
fail in the lists, and passed with him between
those further trees that open Avalon.

They must have fallen, or be falling now,
when that in me which wandered in Provence
is back from pilgrimage alone, and thou
hast closed the lattices that looked on France.

Were they not fallen, they must be falling for ever,
now in the long curves of music—those dead leaves—
as after brass, and the flute's argent quaver,
the oboes die on slow, deciduous breves.

OXFORD

THEY spoke of Spenser at Cambridge, and all the names
of poets that ring her round with a thicket of flames,
and then how Shelley at Oxford sleeps in stone,
beautiful, disillusioned, and alone.

And I felt when I heard them, grey Metropolis
of beauty's legend, as though they had said this
of some woman that I had loved, and thereby proved
that ladies less fair had been more greatly loved.

The fault was mine not yours, who, gazing at you
with the cold unswerving rapture of a statue,
cannot with beauty, like those immortal ones,
impeach the long economy of bronze.

And had I spoken in that lady's defence,
in words that did her wonder violence,
I still were love's reproach, as writing thus
am yours, O greatest poet of all of us.

GENEVA

I RUE DU SOLEIL LEVANT

THERE is no sun that rises anywhere
as reticent as in St. Peter's Square,
till his slow torrent negligently reaches
the slanting thoroughfare behind the beeches,
down which he plunges in a racing flood
to drench the town below with golden mud.
But, when his tide has ebbed, the river-bed
looks back to Calvin with a hint of red,
to shew that you remember how you won
your name, small sister of the rising sun.

GENEVA

II RUE DE TOUTES AMES

STREET of all souls, have in your moonless keeping
these weary souls, who ask no more of you
than that smooth dark, where none awakes from
    sleeping,
and no foot stirs the quiet all night through.

Fold us, for whom there are no walls of jasper,
no gates in heaven, in your dark Order, call
us into your fane, where none cries Matin or Vesper,
and the long Service has no end at all.

THERE are two Gardens. God, who walked in Eden
    with Adam, knew, because of the dark Tree
and the hunger of man for all He has forbidden,
    that the name of the Garden was Gethsemane.

But Christ, who from Gethsemane was taken,
    passing beyond the knowledge of good and evil,
left, as He went, its other name unspoken,
    lest some new Eve should fall to some new devil.

Therefore a sword guards Eden and the Tree,
but there is no angel by Gethsemane.

SPRING WOOD

I wish that I could go back
to Spring Wood below Hawksworth—yes !
I wish I might sleep, and wake
under the branches of those loved trees.
But Bradford lies far away,
and the wood beyond Bradford far ;
and never between night and day,
not under sun, nor cool star,
shall I go back to Bradford,
to Spring Wood below Hawksworth Hall.
There is no way back at evening ;
there is no way back at all.

QUESTION

WHAT SHALL AVAIL US?

WHAT shall avail us at the end of all,
when high things are low things, and great things are
  small ?

What shall avail us, when new is one with old,
when dust is where the eyes were, and the bones lie
  cold ?

What shall avail us, when the light is out,
and the dark from within us meets the dark without ?

What shall avail us, when we lie apart,
and the eternal silence meets the silence in the heart ?

What shall avail us, when all we builded must
blow where the wind blows, and drift with the dust ?

What shall avail us, when beauty suffers wrong,
and love is an echo in a dead poet's song ?

What shall avail us that we were lovers, when
our love is forgotten, or belongs to other men ?

What shall avail us ? Who knows ? Who answers ?
  Wait !
There is no before and after, there is neither small nor
  great,

and the earth is but a shadow, indifferently laid
by the single instant when a heart was unafraid,

by the single moment when a poet or a lover
held out his hands to life, and made it his for ever.

A million, million centuries, a million systems pass,
and death chews upon them, like an idiot chewing
    grass.

They go, but the instant of vision, and the kiss
hold up the torch to God, and God is only this.

THE fool hath said in his heart, " There is no God,"
the fool, that proves by mathematics that he is wiser
than the God who invented him and mathematics,
than the God as visible in a division sum
as in the ravishing division of the lute,
the wise fool, that loves nothing but his folly
in which there is no God.
But God hath said in his heart, " There is no fool,"
and the fool, and his mathematics, and his fourth
    dimension
are not.
But there is another fool, an older fool than Jacques in
    Arden,
the pale fool that some call Pierrot, and others call
lad's-love, that grows in England in the hedges,
and that fool has said in his heart, " There is no death,"
the fool who throws the golden feather of his love
to drift upon the air, but somewhere a king-eagle
has in the mountain-tops fashioned his eyrie
out of gold feathers, and, soaring in the wind,
this last and smallest feather finds the nest,
and the king-eagle hides it with his wings.
And death has said in his heart, " There is no fool,"
but the scarlet wild anemone and the blue grape
    hyacinth
blossom each spring in the valley ; yes, and climb to
    the edge of the snows,
and two or three, perhaps, sturdier than all their
    sisters,
find a little cranny underneath the eagle's eyrie ;
and, one morning, when the king-eagle
rises as though he were tumbling upwards into a star,

he sees, trembling beside his smallest golden feather,
the scarlet wild anemone and the blue grape hyacinth.
For this fool hath said in his heart, "There is no
death "—
and he is right.

AN exquisite dove-coloured bird,
with a throat as soft as a grey glove
on a girl's wrist,
flew with a yellow flick of her wing
across the field of my vision.
She hung for a second in the foreground,
with the level marshes and the sea
like a long grey carpet
behind her.
She had just that fugitive
arrested loveliness of a capital
letter in a missal.
I was terribly contented with my
exquisite dove-coloured bird,
and with the world drained of colour,
as though the wind had sucked it up,
and with the green empty marshes,
and the dull, unadriatic sea.

I wish that my bird
had not suddenly swooped on the ground,
and speared a red worm
with her beak,
as I wish that somebody else's death
were not always the price
of everybody else's life
and of all beauty.

But beauty laid her cool hands on my eyes,
and whispered, " Death

is something that I invented, lest
I should grow tired of myself.
Break me, my poet, so that
I may be born again."

" Yes ! I invented death,"
              beauty saith.

VISION [1]

How lit at what candescent will
ruins the intolerable thrill

that falls in flame, as though it were
the punishment of Lucifer—

the sealing instant when the first
beauty, as though a star had burst

within the spirit, charges it
with some angelic benefit?

One finds it as a boy, in spring,
when the white road is no such thing,

but a white bridge (could heart but span it)
to a new dawn in a new planet.

One finds it when there is no stir
in all the world, and quieter

than falling flakes in fairyland
he finds a hand within his hand.

And some, like Keats, have found it when
a poet swam into their ken,

[1] The first half of this poem was originally written for, and printed
by the Omar Khayyám Club.

91

and changed them with a single word
into the beauty that they heard.

We know not if these starry plans
of ways beyond the world are man's

only, and only, being such,
the proof that he has asked too much

of life, and, therefore, shows by this
his own contrasted frailties.

They may be man's ; but, if they were
a hint at something lovelier

than mind can hold, a hint, a threat
of the unconditioned daysprings, yet

close down the eager heart, lest we
share the gold death of Semele !

It is enough that, for a flash,
fire has overtaken ash,

that life has turned on death, and cried :
" You called me mortal, and you lied."

THE VOYAGERS

" THEY have gone up singing," he said to me.
  " There was a great crowd of them, young and old
    ones.
Devils ! " he said, and then spat suddenly.
  " Ugly they was, but bitter bright, and cold ones."

"What ! up that precipice ? " I asked, " Why not ?
  The likes of them would make the ice ashamed,
wot's laid there since the flood, of being 'ot.
  Devils, they calls them 'ere, and rightly named."

" It's a wild road ! " " What's that to you or me ?
  Leave them to rot. I ain't a going to shout,
not if they kill theirselves, I'm not." " They're free
  of death," I whispered. " Out ! " he screamed. " Get
    out !

I see it in you when you came, the sly
  neat way you munched your food, and wouldn't
    speak.
You're one of them, you are ! " " Alas ! you lie,"
  I said. " They have passed over, I but seek."

" Seek and be damned ! " he muttered, " Or be made
  free of the dream," I answered. A cold chime,
too sweet for voices, thrilled me. Half afraid
  and half enraptured I began to climb.

The crags had torn my hands. Torn were my feet,
  and all my body reeled with climbing pain,
and the wild world was muffled with the beat
  of driving mist, and hail, and slanting rain.

Still I climbed on, for, if I stopped, below
  the serried rocks, and far above me, plain
between the glacier and the streaming snow,
  a chimney-path across the black moraine.

Nothing to do but climb, until night came,
  and then, unless I found them, I should lie
with all the others, who had seen the flame,
  and watched it, as the darkness choked them, die.

Came then a little pause in the wind. The mist
  half-lifted, and I saw, all pain forgetting,
the great sun wheel a blade of amethyst,
  and slap it back into the scabbard, setting.

So then the moon walked smoothly on the snows,
  outsilvering their silver, and I said,
" Moonlight and death!" and one replied, "Who goes,
  living, between the moonlight and the dead ? "

I never saw their face, nor knew what hands
  lifted me into safety, what warm wind,
blowing from what deep lemon-haunted lands,
  made all the midnight fragrant, hushed, and kind.

94

I never spoke with them, nor save that once
    did any speak with me, and yet it seemed
that all my thoughts, as through a flute of bronze,
    were moulded into words I had not dreamed.

And when I woke I lay among the firs,
    with the peaks far above, and all I had
for climbing and disaster this poor verse,
    that (as it seemed) in dreaming I had made.

THE SONG

If that is a sword, break it !
    If that is hatred, go !
Here is life as we would make it,
    where none can say us " No."

You have brought silver, crude as
    the first who sold his Lord.
Throw down the pieces, Judas,
    as idle as the sword !

You nothing knew ? Make fast your
    soul to what no one knows !
Here is the upland pasture,
    green at the edge of the snows.

95

No guide to lead, or only
    the peak that none has trod.
Who goes with us, goes lonely
    between his soul and God.

We have found peace, not your peace
    but the eagles' peace as they hover,
a terrible bright, unsure peace,
    of the lover that has no lover.

Go back and say you have seen us
    with no shadow before or behind,
save the shadow of your God between us
    and the God that we go to find.

THESE things Odysseus : " Tie me to the mast.
I'll hear that song the Sirens have at last.
I am not afraid of women, nor the sound
of voices that still the water with the wound
of loveliness. I have not sailed the seas,
and known in the heart the wooing silences
and the storms tossed in those long green arms, to
    shrink
at a song, although it shiver on the brink
of the spirit, like the third wave, holding back
for one green airless second ere it crack.
I have seen strange sights since last I saw the sun
die red in Ithaca, on Neriton.
Monsters I have fought, through terror clambered
into release, and with the gods have chambered
till my mind has been woven into a shining stuff
like the shadow a god throws. It is not enough
for a man to have seen Helen dip the moon
with her white arms, and to have watched a city
    swoon
into flame for her beauty, and the cracking towers
thrown at her feet, a garland of red flowers,
and she, as these blossoms perished one by one,
shone in the gloom, white rose of Ilion.
It is not enough to have seen this, unless
the soul admitted to that great loveliness,
and, thus bereft, should toss this trifling breath,
like the two coins flung casually to death,
and crush the Sirens by the throat till they tell
how, though Poseidon make the heavens spill,
to lick the seas up with a roaring lip,
swallowing like spent foam our fellowship,

the dominant peril beyond the utmost West
is beauty recovered, and the heart at rest.
The Sirens have that knowledge. It is well
that one should share it, and should live to tell,
if there are words to frame it ; or, if speech
should be too small, then that one heart should reach
out of mortality, to tremble where
great Zeus himself is but a listener
to an older godhead that outgods his own,
and sees behind his throne a greater throne."

And all the time the Queen Penelope
watched for Odysseus sailing home, but he
tore at the ropes with which his men had bound him,
and wept for the song of the Sirens, dying round him.

WHAT THE SIRENS SANG

ONLY a harp breaking, only a broken harp,
but the world is shaking with a sudden sharp
sound of dreams rending, as though life were,
in the moment of ending, lovelier
than youth, than bridal, than the kiss of the lover ;
and death, like a tidal wave, sweeps over,
with release for the sailor in her long green kisses,

and the world grows paler than the girl, Ulysses,
than the girl on the coast of youth's memory—
the pitiful ghost of Penelope.
Death's voice is the same as her voice was (oh,
      Captain)
that night when it came as a star you were rapt in,
when it rose and you heard then, in a world stricken
      dumb,
love whisper the word then we are whispering—
      " Come ! "

WHAT AM I AFRAID FOR?

My heart is beating. But what am I afraid for?
It was not ourselves, my heart, that you and I were
    made for.

Long since—listen!—we saw happiness
like a girl standing in her first ball-dress,
standing by the window at the foot of the stair,
and the black night behind her like a ribbon in her hair.
Yes, and the fiddles. Yes, and the cold flute,
that took us in the aeroplane that has no parachute,
and called to us above the clouds, " Well ! isn't this
    romance ? "
But, when we stepped out on the air, we found we
    couldn't dance.

(O fiddles calling, O cold flute,
what does it matter now that you are mute,
now that the delicate drift and thrill
of powdered music is utterly still ?
What does it matter to a dead demirep
that we could have waltzed to heaven, if we'd had one
    dancing-step ?)

My heart is lonely. But what am I afraid for?
Loneliness is surely what the poet's heart is made for.

Long since—listen !—we saw friendship stand,
holding the future like an apple in his hand,
holding it, and tossing it, and laughing very sweet,
as though it were the apple that Adam had to eat.
Well ! what an apple ! Well ! what a Tree !
Unbar the gate of Eden, and let me go free.
Aye ! there are golden crowns in Eden, but,
ere we win that crown again, there are other crowns
     to cut.

(O subtle serpent, O apple round,
what do you matter now I have found,
now that I am tempting you
with knowledge Eden never knew.
What does it matter, when a lad can sing,
if God walks with another in the cool of evening ?)

My heart is broken. What am I afraid for ?
Pain is the leit-motif every tune is played for.

Long since—listen ! O reed of my desire !
I set your slimness to my lips. My lips were touched
     with fire.
All the stars in heaven went singing to the south,
and the singing constellations were the kisses of your
     mouth.
Well ! my heart is broken ! Well ! my eyes are black,
but I fashion out of darkness a greater Zodiac,
inky stars blotting heaven sign by sign,
but every star the shadow of a darker thought of mine.

(O stars faded, O love shared,
what does it matter, now that I have dared,
now that I have walked alone
with my own unguessed unknown,
that happiness, and friendship, and the heart that was
    hers
are only the skeletons at the marriage-feast of verse?)

PERSONS

MARY STUART said to Darnley, "Nay, do not scold me!
Not my fault, but your fault, that you could not hold
  me.
I came out of France into Scotland, hearing
the faint, cold sound of the Morte in the forest-clearing,
and now when the air is wild with it, and they rend me,
what in your love has turned on the hounds to defend
  me?
No, you have flinched like the rest, while my throat is
  torn,
Darnley, and your love is the last high note of the horn.
Go back to the King, and tell him Mary has told you
that she would have given the world to be held—as she
  did not hold you."

But Darnley did not speak. He looked at her, where she
  stood
by the thick, grey wall of her castle Holyrood,
and he saw the long dykes behind her, the lake that
  still is
red in the dreams of her lovers with her water-lilies;
and he saw the white swans, as these lovers have seen
also, in dreams, the white shoulders of their queen,
and before they have the desire of their eyes, they wake,
and their hearts are cold within them, for the white
  shoulders' sake.
So Darnley turned away from her, only keeping
in his ears the sound of a fish from the water leaping.

But Mary, the daughter of France, the pale Queen's
    daughter,
watched another queen, and a stranger, in the still
    water—
a quieter queen than Mary, a queen more cool,
as pale as frail as Mary, but not more beautiful,
till the night comes up where no one sees, or has seen,
Mary the Queen of Scotland, and her sister, the water-
    queen.

BAUDELAIRE, I wish that I could learn from you
   how, on the words, to make a chisel pounce,
and smash a hammer till the shape came through
   like some Greek runner struggling out of bronze.
I wish, like you, that I could make my line
   cool as a statue, and yet subtly warm
with something even you could not divine
   until it flashed, and took your heart by storm.
Smooth and deliberate with the classic curve,
   resolving the mute obstinacy of metal,
your enigmatic masterpieces swerve
   out of the climate of sound, and, swaying a little,
compose themselves with the conclusive air
of dominated marble, Baudelaire.

Don't flash your bull's eye on me. I'm all right.
I shan't do nothing wrong—nor I'm not lost
nor drunk. You've seen me 'ere before at night?
Quite likely! Well, who am I? I'm a ghost.
Haunting? Well, 'ardly (Hardly I should say),
but as to bein' dead, well, who'll deny
he'll not come back again, not Folkestone way—
Art Kipps—the shop assistant—who was I.
You'd 'ardly guess how lonely Heaven can be,
constable—for a chap who has no use
for all this business of immortality,
and those dark trees in the long avenues!
It's like a church—only this difference—
the saints 'as left the windows, and the bells
are always ringing, and you've got the sense
that all you see and 'ear means something else.
I'm puzzled in Heaven. See? I am. It's not
what I've been used to. Makes me want to come
badly—to see poor Buggins, and his lot,
tidying up the old Emporium.
I've thought of them when swells with some great name
'ave spoken to me—not that they are proud,
but swells and me can never be the same;
I want to be along of my old crowd.
My sort don't suit with immortality.
It hurts, does living after death—it's wrong—
I want to rest with other chaps like me—
Must you be going! Well, ole chep—so long.

MICHAEL COLLINS

August 24th, 1922

" THEY have killed Michael Collins,"
thinks the old grey ghost of Parnell.
" But you were killed at thirty-three, Michael,
in battle ; you died well.

There was no breaking of an old heart for ye,
nor pointing of the finger, and slow shame,
and a boy saying to another : ' Is that he—
Parnell, that had the high name ? '

You'll not be hearing, Michael, Michael,
Ireland going away, as I do,
and her soft feet quiet in the distance—
Michael ! It's me they've killed again, not you."

You have said : " Who could have foretold
that the heart grows old ? "
You have said it, whose wild swans beat
into the immortal heat
of the world, where Shelley waits
with your laurel, Yeats.

But, though you outlive desire,
bend by the fire
you lit for a lady, and then
kindle your heart again,
as she, at the bars,
with the blood of the stars.

What is that blood ? It does not start,
like the poor stuff in the heart,
out of a broken vein ;
it does not tarnish nor stain ;
is thinner than water is ;
it has no depth or degrees,
and it does not find its level,
for it flows between god and devil.

It is quiet, where the embers glisten ;
poet, listen
to the curlew that will
be crying over the hill
always, as you know best,
to your waters of the West.

And if, as I think, you hear
still in the cloudless air
the pinions beating on,
and the voice of the passing swan,
I could have guessed, could have told,
why the heart grows old.

For you remembered the spring,
and song awakening,
as a thorn, lost in the snows,
might dream of her rose,
till almost the snowflakes were
a petalled ghost of her ;
but she wakes and the rose is gone.
Yeats, dream on !

WOMEN

I HAVE heard men speak of women—
pale swan-women, princesses of the story,
so that against their smooth and sloping breasts
you could almost see the shadow of the feathers ;
eagle-women, striking down suddenly
out of clear air, but these were very lovely
in the savage blackness of their stooping wings ;
nightingale-women, who pass by singing
(between midnight and dawn, between sound and
    silence),
" Itylus, Itylus," and only the sorrow remains ;
and dove-women, folding their grey plumage
like a veil about them, like a nun's soft cowl,
and bending their meek heads, as though they heard
always, far off and lovely, angelus—
till the whole room was full of wings,
swan-wings, eagle-wings, wings of the nightingale,
and that chimed benediction of the dove.
And among all these women I have thought of you,
not winged, like those, nor asking, like those, for wings,
nor seeking to be among women that are praised,
but standing alone, looking fearlessly at life,
not hoping to lure or smooth or frighten her,
but gravely holding out a steady hand,
as to another woman like yourself,
having no tricks, save only the one trick
of courage, and the will to stand alone.

HE has put by,
departing hence,
his beauty's high
inheritance.

Yet we'll not blame
death, since we knew him,
and beauty came
upon us through him.

A candle cool
he was—in us
beautiful,
and luminous.

You come swiftly down on the wind, O runners,
cutting the obstinate swathes of space
with the long easy motion of the scythe,
trailing your speed behind you, like banners,
and as you draw effortless to the end of the race,
stooping a little as though to gather the swathe.

What is better than, with forehead lifted, O runners,
to speed clean out of the darkness in the mind
into bright uplands of motion beyond desire ?
Gatherers of the flowers of distance, passionate gleaners
through the invisible silver cornlands of the wind,
you are not boys running, you are life breaking free,
    you are fire !

In a coco-
nut, two thin
tapers burn
a line of green.
That's the mandril.
Now, eyes shut
leave a red, dead
coco-nut.
Algol above me
blazes; then
suddenly is
dim again.
The mandril's shifting
beacons are
also
a variable star.

LILITH

You had black hair, Lilith, and the great snake
learned from black snakes in your hair his coilèd art,
for God, when he made his Eden, forgot to make
barriers against beauty's serpents in the heart.

And what do the later shapes of beauty spell
but pale repeated smiles, diverted frowns,
that in your darkness unrepeatable
were beauty's first adjectives, and love's first nouns ?

And that, in our tears and laughter, outreaching these
is but an echo of your sorrowless mirth,
that broke upon the Paradisal peace
with the primitive derisions of the earth.

You had black hair, Lilith, and when those two—
Adam and Eve—were from their Eden driven,
the serpent was caught in your black hair, and you
laughed, and God heard your laughter, and wept in
    heaven.

THE ALPINE CROSS

CHRIST, on Your Alpine Cross, beautiful, pale, and
    young,
faded long since are the flowers You suffered among,
but the blossom of the snow, quietly drifting down,
has hidden with silver mercy the thorns of Your crown.

The cool hands of the frost have mended Your feet and
    side,
stanching the wounds of Your Passion with pitiful ice.
You stretch Your arms in a sleep, as though You had
    never died.
as though You had never lost nor regained a Paradise.

SONNETS

As in the shadowed Alpine aisles a birch,
  lost in a marching wood of pines and firs,
tosses in the wind her bright hair, like a torch
  against the dark, and claims all spring for hers—
so by the wind, in dream that only whispers,
  beckoned, youth claims the world, his gauntlet
    flinging
to age, the organist surprised at Vespers
  by the silver mutiny of a boy singing.   *Lovely line*
Youth sees against the skyline the same hill
  that all have seen, nor knowing, if he cross,
  he will but find himself grown old beyond,
goes, as all go, and the world becomes so still,
  you can almost hear the raindrop in the moss,
  and a great lily tremble in the pond.

Poets, hereafter when our books are read,
    will any speak for us ? Who will reply
    when of all those who should be damned and dead
this is not damned, and that one will not die ?
Will it be Wisdom poring through his glasses
    that ranks us, or the voice of some great school ?
    Or will some lady, light upon the grasses
as she we sung, and not less beautiful,
cry for us to the world : " But this was spent,
    and that went crying for what he did not have,
    and could so great a want have been content
with the small satisfactions of the grave ?
    For he remains, while all the rest pass over
    who was a poet too, but first a lover."

THE JAPANESE MASK

WHAT had you in your mind, artificer,
    that made you carve that little mask of slumber?
    Was it imagined beauty, or did you remember
some woman's face, and move your hands to her
through bronze, as once against her hair and cheek?
    Those deep, slant eyes—never, when you were near,
    did they close so? and that shell-slender ear—
did the hair hide it thus when you would speak?
And then those cold unkissable lips—no doubt
    there were lips once—ah, softer lips and wetter
    with your tears on them than this perfect, bitter
mouth, that you carved, I think, when love went out.
    But, if you lost, and moulded her in your grief,
    she is yours now beyond the heart's belief.

ABSENCE

How should not absence from thy presence change me,
    since in thy presence all my future is,
and in thy absence all that doth estrange me
    from that, and binds me to past miseries ?
I, like a shadow, when the lighted candle
    is snuffed, into a little pool of black
shrink in a second, but, if you rekindle
    your flame, then on the instant I am back.
O my bright candle, since it is your virtue
    and use to shine, and set your shadow moving,
shine, well assured that naught in him can hurt you,
    and least his small and ghostly way of loving.
Ghosts with God's word are laid, but mine with less,
who only need for that a woman's " yes."

THE STAR

I AM her thought, and she, who this conceivèd,
    has, being absent, turned her mind away,
so that I glimmer too faint to be aggrievèd,
    too fugitive to scold, and so must stay
until her quickening beam revolve, and, seeing
    all dark that was with her reflection lit,
she, in the greatness of her starry being,
    sets this aflame, and makes a star of it.
For all her thoughts are stars, that hang unguessed
    through the light-years of beauty, till they stir
some night of wonder and rising in his breast,
    all dark—astound love's pale astronomer.
Therefore, be still, my heart ! You nothing are
now, but may be, as once you were, a star.

SURE, you were God's first general election,
  and, when life's warring atoms were all rent
with hatred and with blindness, healed the faction
  with beauty's re-established government.
Then was there peace for old dreams, walking slowly
  like old men in the evening of their days ;
then was there joy of youth enfranchised wholly,
  and for the poet who had failed, the bays.
You organised the summer so that dearth
  with some green riches rustled into corn,
and, where death's tenements had crushed the earth,
  you cleared the slums, and loveliness was born,
confirming with the suffrage of a flower
from spring to spring your tenancy of power.

THE POET'S SECRET

I WILL tell you the poet's secret. It is this :
   to trap the shadow and leave the light that cast it,
to set a sound beside those silences
   that give the sound its glory and outlast it.
There is a net of colour at the edge of the mind,
   and the poet beats against it, as a bird
against a stained-glass window, but, behind
   the window, distance stainless, cold, unstirred.
The poet is a prince who is not crowned,
   but stand in silence where the poet stands,
and you shall almost hear high trumpets sound,
   beyond the world, the laying on of hands !
Be very still, and you shall share the holy
balsam of beauty, in dark descending slowly.

ALL men are heirs to riches. They inherit
  a vast estate the day that they draw breath.
They, by the right of Eve and Adam's merit,
  assume the feudal policies of death.
Their actions wear his livery. Their thought
  is the tradition of his *seigneurie*.
Their dreams are heirlooms, and their love is naught
  but whispers and his fleeting memory.
But some refuse their heritage. These owe
  dangerous fealty to life, the lord
that lights them home, by ways death does not know,
  to Eden by the flashes of his sword—
the poets from the riches of the dead
magnificently disinherited.

FIRST LOVE

First love is love before the flame is lit ;
   it is the waking bird, before the rest
on cool wet branch, all drowsy-green with it,
   and sinking back to silence in the nest.
First love has more of art and less of wit
   than later love, wherein are manifest
the brain and mind in balance exquisite,
   where good in each becomes completed best.
And there the spirit, that has half remembered
   and half forgotten that life, asking all,
gives twice what it demands, sweeps unencumbered
   sheer into love, as when a waterfall
tumbles, all white, into the sun that dies on
the grave, incontrovertible horizon.

J'ÉCOUTE TES YEUX

HAVE I not heard all April in your eyes,
 seen in your voice the snowdrop in the snow?
Has not your laughter made my folly wise,
 your wisdom taught me what I need not know?
Have I not, standing dream-bound at your side,
 outpaced this dusty planet, to discover
that swifter world than fire, where the bride
 holds out her hands in silence to the lover?
For thus the senses shift because of you,
 as though an angel, singing to a lute,
did with some trick of harmony endue
 each with the other's dearest attribute.
And life and death, by that angelic grace,
are light and shadow, changing in your face.

Lovely

PSYCHE

IF love were only to see and to desire
   the things of earth that were desirable,
till the last ash of the heart has spent its fire,
   there were no tale of the spent heart to tell.
But love is not content with that. Love seeks
   to make a man and woman in his own image,
forgetting the ache of wings, and how man speaks
   in mortal accent love's immortal damage.
Yes ! love would have us gods, and he would stamp us
   with the high shapes of heaven, and, for a sign,
we carry in our hearts some lost Olympus,
   cold as the stone beyond the furthest pine.
Earth is enough to suffer. Must we be
the frightened hosts of immortality ?

For all we sought and missed, or left unclaimed,
  for all the dreams we had and lost, for youth,
ruffling his hair, suppled by Time, and tamed,
  for love denied, or seen with too much truth,
for faith, like a sword, with long misprision rusted,
  for all adventure, before the quest is ended,
abandoned or betrayed, for beauty misted
  by the half-lights of vision, for pity attended
with the bitterness of those who take and give,
  for heavens, that had they been accessible,
  were heavens only by the side of hell,
for all of us who die, before we live,
  for all the crippled feet on the long road
  you made for angels, we forgive you, God.

VALEDICTION

THE PIT

In the Pit there was a poet crying,
" Heaven," but the devil said,
" Fool ! have done with your lying,
now that you are dead !

' Heaven ! ' and the hands you wrote with
shrivel, and the words crash
into dust, and fill your throat with
this calcinated ash."

But the poet answered " Devil !
Ashes and fire and death
and darkness, and all things evil
are the breath of the poet's breath.

And when the rest are stricken
in this your hell, and cringe,
the poet's senses quicken ;
and, smashing back the hinge

on which your sodden portal
is bolted, barred, and slammed,
his song becomes immortal,
because his soul is damned."

AN EASTERN COURT

" And not to wake "

Here, quiet and long peace,
   shadows of the shade
of which life's mysteries,
   and men are made,

gather, drift and unfold
   into the swift, proud
death of the sun in gold
   on the last cloud.

Only to die in fire,
   flake after flake—
and to outburn desire—
   and not to wake.

THEN why should a man complain
because of a little pain?
His heart that burns so hot
will be cold enough, and rot
at his allotted term,
with the slow incessant worm.

He will not be wise nor brave,
nor a lover, in the grave,
and he will not know nor care
what wind blows through what hair,
what pointed hands are narrow,
when they fold, as a pointed arrow.

And, if peace be such precious stuff,
he will have peace enough
to bottom the pouring Pit
with a tenth of his share of it,
to smother Time, and still
have eternity to spill.

God send him a pain to hug,
when the cool, immediate drug
of death has healed the fever,
which is man's birthright, for ever,
and a bone rubs on a bone,
and not even these his own.

IF you remember me, remember me only
    as a voice once heard singing, as a cry.
I will go down to the darkness lonely
    with my heart, when I die.

Let those who write of me say, " None knew him ! "
    Let those who speak of me curtly say : " This
was slight as a reed, and the wind went through him
    at its cool will, not his."

What is it to you then, that I have suffered,
    that I have loved, was loved, that I paltered or lied ?
Here in my verse is the thing that I offered.
    The man has died.

Now in these fairylands
gather your weary hands
close to your breast,
and be at rest.

Now in these silences
lean to the cadences,
moulding their grace
to the line of your face.

Now at the end of all,
loveliest friend of all,
all these things are yours,
in this peace that endures.

SHALL I break my rhythms now, shall I bid them
　remember the earth and the low nest,
creep now where once the grasses hid them,
　have done with wings, be at rest?

Come back to the earth that once they rose from,
　come back, be folded, breathe
the cold indifferent air that flows from
　the fruitless dark beneath?

Leave them to lie between the sullen
　stems of the grasses, and to settle
without a sound where they have fallen
　into the dust, below the nettle.

Let them crumble there until the grasses
　sway above them, and they do not stir,
growing, as the dream they failed of passes,
　quieter and quieter.

SOFTLY out of a dream
   there is a voice crying :
" Where I am
   is no modifying
of beauty, no
   compromise
in honour's—oh,
   how perilous—eyes,
no dimming of the vision,
   no blade that tilts,
but only God's compassion,
   and your kiss on the hilts."

TAILPIECE

BRIGHT hair, grow dim ;
   close, slender hands,
for the long dream
   till the world ends.

No wind to ruffle,
   no pain to wring,
now she may baffle
   everything.

Grow dim, bright hair !
   Hands, close for ever !
So she was fair ;
   So let us leave her.